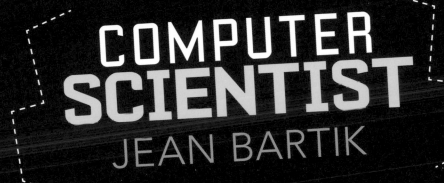

COMPUTER
SCIENTIST
JEAN BARTIK

JENNIFER REED

Lerner Publications ◆ Minneapolis

Lerner Publications Company
A division of Lerner Publishing Group, Inc.
241 First Avenue North
Minneapolis, MN 55401 U.S.A.

For reading levels and more information, look up this title at www.lernerbooks.com.

Content Consultant: Kim D. Todd, Assistant Director, Jean Jennings Bartik Computing Museum, Northwest Missouri State University

Library of Congress Cataloging-in-Publication Data

The Cataloging-in-Publication Data for *Computer Scientist Jean Bartik* is on file at the Library of Congress.
ISBN 978-1-5124-0789-1 (lib. bdg.)
ISBN 978-1-5124-1310-6 (pbk.)
ISBN 978-1-5124-1092-1 (EB pdf)

Manufactured in the United States of America
1 – PC – 7/15/16

The images in this book are used with the permission of: © Mark Summerfield/Alamy Stock Photo, p. 4; © 1938–39 Stanberry High School Year Book, Courtesy of the Jennings Bartik Computing Museum, Northwest Missouri State University, and the Stanberry School R-II District. Used with Permission., p. 5; © Mirrorpix/Newscom, p. 7; © Courtesy of the Jean Jennings Bartik Computing Museum and the Northwest Missouri State University Archives. Used with Permission., p. 8; © 2002 Jean Jennings Bartik Computing Museum, Northwest Missouri State University. Used with Permission., pp. 9, 10; © akg-images/Newscom, pp. 11, 23; US Army photo from the archives of the ARL Technical Library, courtesy of the Jean Jennings Bartik Computing Museum, Northwest Missouri State University., pp. 13, 15, 19; © Science Source, p. 14; US Army Photo, p. 16; © Bettmann/Corbis, pp. 20, 22; © Underwood Archives/UIG Universal Images Group/Newscom, p. 21; © Heritage Image Partnership Ltd/Alamy Stock Photo, p. 25; University Photographer Darren Whitley. © 2002 Jean Jennings Bartik & University Marketing and Communications, Northwest Missouri Stated University. All rights Reserved. Used with Permission., p. 26; Dr. Jon T. Rickman, Vice President of Information Technology. © 2008 Jean Jennings Bartik Computing Museum, Northwest Missouri State University. Used with Permission., p. 27.

Front Cover: Jean Jennings Bartik, ca. 1941. © 2002 Jean Jennings Bartik Computing Museum, Northwest Missouri State University. Used with permission.

CONTENTS

Growing up, Betty Jean Jennings attended a one-room schoolhouse similar to this one in Point Lookout, Missouri.

MATH STAR

Betty Jean Jennings was born on a farm in Missouri in 1924, and she had big dreams. Her father was a teacher and a farmer. Her mother was a homemaker. Betty Jean was the sixth of seven children. As a young girl, Betty Jean dreamed of being an independent woman one day. She wanted to stand out in the world.

Betty Jean went to school in a one-room schoolhouse. Students in the first through eighth grades were taught together. Whenever she finished her own work, Betty Jean liked to listen to lessons being taught to the upper grades. This helped her learn even more.

Betty Jean especially loved math. She was very good at it. Her teacher suggested that Betty Jean combine fifth and sixth grade math into one year. Betty Jean skipped a grade.

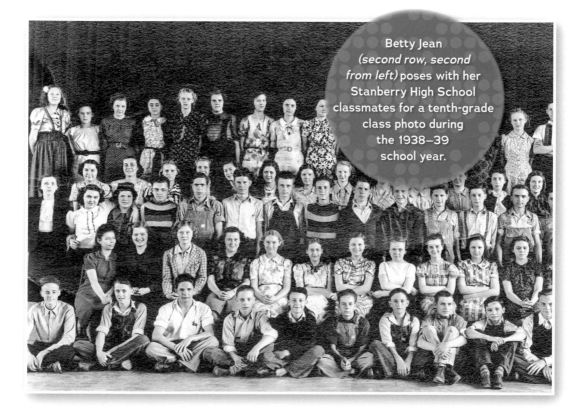

Betty Jean (second row, second from left) poses with her Stanberry High School classmates for a tenth-grade class photo during the 1938–39 school year.

After completing eighth grade, Betty Jean enrolled in Stanberry High School in 1937. She decided she wanted to become a nurse. At the time, there were not many opportunities for women who loved math. But nurses use addition, subtraction, fractions, and ratios to figure out how much medicine to give to a patient. They also use math every day when recording vital signs. Betty Jean liked the idea of helping others. With this goal in mind, Betty Jean and her favorite teacher, Miss Madeira, studied Latin together, since many medical terms used Latin.

TECH TALK

"Lots of medical terms are derived from Latin, so I decided to study Latin, which wasn't offered by the school. However, Miss Madeira came to my rescue, offering to refresh her Latin and study it with me. I went over to Miss Madeira's house one night a week, and sometimes after our lessons, Miss Madeira would listen with kind understanding and encouragement to my fantasies and ambitions."

—Jean Bartik

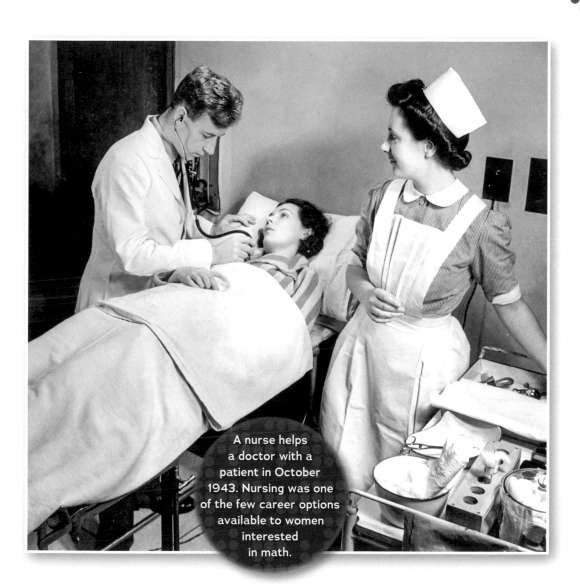

A nurse helps a doctor with a patient in October 1943. Nursing was one of the few career options available to women interested in math.

Betty Jean graduated from high school in 1941. She was just sixteen years old. She was the second-best pupil in the school, and she also earned the highest mathematics grades anyone had ever received at the school.

Chapter 2

After high school, Jennings attended Northwest Missouri State Teachers College.

HUMAN COMPUTERS

College offered Jennings the opportunity to leave home and start her adventure. She attended Northwest Missouri State Teachers College (now Northwest Missouri State University) in Maryville, Missouri. But she no longer wanted to be a nurse. She decided to major in mathematics with a minor in English.

During Jennings's first year in college, the United States entered World War II (1939–1945). Japanese aircraft attacked the US naval base in Pearl Harbor, Hawaii, in December 1941, drawing the United States into the war. Because of the war, many men were drafted into the military. Most of the students remaining at Jennings's college were women. However, the US Navy set up a program at her college and sent hundreds of sailors there for training. Jennings took math and science classes such as calculus, trigonometry, and physics with these sailors. She was the only woman in the classes.

Jennings *(left)* and her college roommate, Virginia McGinness, lived on Fourth Street in Maryville, Missouri.

Jennings chats with one of the men enrolled in the US Navy program at Northwest Missouri State University.

Jennings graduated in 1945. She was the only person from her college to graduate with a degree in math that year. Jennings did not yet know what she was going to do with her math degree.

With many of the nation's men fighting overseas, women were taking over jobs that had previously only been held by men. This was especially true for jobs related to technology. Women served as code breakers and machine operators. These jobs were all classified work. This meant they were top secret. The women who performed these jobs were known as the Top Secret Rosies.

A woman packs cartridges at a factory in Philadelphia, Pennsylvania, during World War II. Women who did defense work during the war were often referred to as "Rosies."

TECH TALK

"A computer wasn't a machine. It was a person. . . . Mathematics was a crucial weapon of the US arsenal, and women, its secret practitioners."

—LeAnn Erickson, director of a documentary on the Top Secret Rosies

Jennings heard the military was hiring math majors to be "computers." In the 1940s, the word *computer* referred to workers who performed calculations by hand. These workers were often women. They worked long hours doing mathematical calculations. Jennings applied for a job as a computer for the United States Department of War and was hired.

The US Department of War assigned Jennings to work at the **Ballistics** Research Lab at the University of Pennsylvania. There she calculated ballistics for military weapons. These calculations determined how far and how fast a bullet or missile would go when shot. This information allowed the military to aim their weapons at specific targets.

Computers Kay McNulty (*left*) and Alyse Snyder use a differential analyzer at the University of Pennsylvania to calculate ballistics during World War II. The differential analyzer was a type of mechanical analog computer.

Although her work was important to the war effort, Jennings grew tired of doing the repetitive calculations. She was ready for a new adventure. In 1945 Jennings applied to work on a new top-secret military project.

Chapter 3

The ENIAC was the first general-purpose electronic computer.

THE ENIAC

In June 1945, Jennings was one of six women hired as **programmers** for a newly developed **computer** called the Electronic Numerical Integrator and Computer (ENIAC). All six of them had majored in math. They knew how to run numbers on a calculator, but the ENIAC was quite different. For one thing, it took up almost an entire room. It stood nearly 9 feet (2.7 meters) tall. It stretched 80 feet (24 m) in length, and it weighed 30 tons (27 metric tons). It was faster and more reliable than a human computer. But it was still in its infancy.

The ENIAC was developed at the Moore School of Electrical Engineering at the University of Pennsylvania by John Mauchly and John Presper Eckert. It was the first general-purpose electronic computer. This means it could be used to complete many different types of calculations. The military wanted to use the machine to calculate ballistics faster and more reliably than humans could do by hand. But Mauchly and Eckert had designed the computer to solve many other problems as well.

Two of the original six programmers, Ruth Lichterman *(left)* and Marlyn Wescoff, work on the ENIAC.

Programmers Jennings (*left*) and Frances Bilas operate the ENIAC at its main control panel.

The ENIAC could solve problems one thousand times faster than any other computing machine of its time. It had forty individual panels that performed different functions. It contained twenty **accumulators**, which could add and subtract. Each of the accumulators could also hold a ten-digit decimal number in **memory**.

Jennings and her colleagues first had to figure out how the ENIAC worked. But they had to learn how it worked without ever seeing the actual machine. The ENIAC was so top secret that very few people had high enough clearance to see the computer in action. The programmers examined diagrams of the ENIAC's circuits. And Mauchly answered any questions they came up with along the way. Then World War II ended when Japan surrendered in September 1945. In October Jennings and her fellow programmers were allowed to see the ENIAC for the first time. Jennings and her colleague Betty Snyder finally began to program the ENIAC to calculate ballistics for the military.

On February 15, 1946, Mauchly, Eckert, and the six programmers shared the ENIAC with the world. They gave a formal demonstration of Jennings and Snyder's program to the scientific community. The demonstration was a success. It proved to the world that the ENIAC was the first computer to successfully run a program.

TECH TALK

"We were thrilled to see the ENIAC for the first time and amazed by its size. It was much bigger and more magnificent and intimidating than we had imagined."

—Jean Bartik

In the fall of 1946, the ENIAC was moved from the University of Pennsylvania to Aberdeen Proving Ground in Maryland. Jennings and others continued to improve it. In December of that year, Jennings also married Bill Bartik and began using her husband's last name.

In December 1946, Bartik was asked to lead a team to turn the ENIAC into a stored-program computer. The first computers could only be wired to run one program at a time. In order to run a new program, the computers had to be rewired. By the end of March 1948, Bartik's team had figured out how to increase the ENIAC's memory. That meant the ENIAC could store different program instructions in its memory. The ENIAC continued operating until October 2, 1955. Over the years, it was used for many purposes, including weather prediction and research on the design of wind tunnels.

TECH TALK

"We had tamed a mechanical beast and made it purr."
—*Jean Bartik, discussing the successful programming of the ENIAC*

Mauchly (*front left*), Jennings (*back left*), and other members of the ENIAC team operate the machine in 1946.

Chapter 4

Eckert demonstrates the UNIVAC in 1951.

WELL-DESERVED
RECOGNITION

After the success of converting the ENIAC to a stored-program computer, Bartik began working for the Eckert-Mauchly Computer Corporation, a private company formed by Eckert and Mauchly after World War II. There,

Bartik helped program a new computer, the Universal Automatic Computer (UNIVAC) I. The UNIVAC could quickly do simple math problems, and it could also store words. This made it easier for businesses to use the computer for a wider variety of tasks, such as keeping track of inventory. While working on it, she wrote the world's first sort/merge program

The UNIVAC was the first commercial computer produced in the United States.

for a computer. Sort/merge programs allow computers to break down large pieces of data into smaller, more manageable pieces.

Eckert-Mauchly Computer Corporation was acquired by Remington Rand Inc. in 1950. Many employees, including Bartik, continued working for Remington Rand. In 1951 they sold the

After the success of the 1950 population census, workers used the UNIVAC to tabulate the entire 1954 economic census.

first UNIVAC to the United States Census Bureau to help calculate the 1950 US census.

While working on the UNIVAC, Bartik also programmed the Binary Automatic Computer (BINAC), a computer used by Northrop Aircraft. The BINAC was designed to control long-range missiles. It consisted of two identical computers

The BINAC undergoes a test run at the manufacturer in 1949.

that did the same tasks, double-checking each calculation in the process.

Even though Bartik was a successful computer programmer, it was difficult for her to get any recognition for her work. The same year Remington Rand purchased Eckert-Mauchly, Bartik was scheduled to give a presentation to one of its customers, the Naval Aviation Supply Office. But as the date for the meeting drew nearer, Remington Rand decided a man should give the presentation to the navy commanders instead. Bartik only delivered a proposal at the end of the meeting. After the presentation, Bartik wasn't allowed to attend dinner with the men because they thought she might be offended by their jokes. Remington Rand never allowed Bartik to give another presentation.

Bartik decided to leave Remington Rand in 1951. She dedicated the next sixteen years to raising her three children. She also went back to school. In August 1967 she received a master's degree in English from the University of Pennsylvania.

After completing her degree, Bartik decided to rejoin the workforce. However, she discovered that jobs for women in the computer science world were hard to come by. In addition, computers were now completely different than they had been when she first began her career. They had become much

Two employees work in the computer room of Huntsman House in 1968. By the late 1960s, computers had gotten smaller and faster.

Bartik (right) and fellow ENIAC programmer Kay McNulty Mauchly Antonelli display a component of the ENIAC at the University of Pennsylvania in 2002.

smaller. They could process and store information much faster and better than computers such as the ENIAC ever could.

So, instead of programming, Bartik wrote and edited publications about computers and the computer science industry. She worked for Auerbach Corporation, Honeywell, and Data Decisions. And she also had another mission. She fought for the recognition of women in technology and the workplace.

Bartik encouraged women in the field of computing. She gave many talks to women in college and in the computer industry.

Bartik also received awards recognizing her as a pioneering programmer. In 2002 the Jean Jennings Bartik Computing Museum opened at Northwest Missouri State University. In 2008 the Computer History Museum in Mountain View, California, granted Bartik the Museum Fellows Award. That same year, Bartik received the Institute of Electrical and

The Computer History Museum is dedicated to preserving artifacts related to the history of computing. The museum inducted Bartik *(center)* into their Hall of Fellows in 2008.

TECH TALK

"I think you should be prepared, and work hard—everybody that succeeds must work hard—and open the door when opportunity knocks. Opportunity comes in a lot of different ways. But I do believe that you should enjoy what you do."

—Jean Bartik, offering advice to young women entering the field of computer science

Electronics Engineers Computer Pioneer Award. It honored her pioneering efforts as one of the first computer programmers.

In 2011, Bartik died of congestive heart disease. She left behind an important legacy. At a time when women were not encouraged to pursue careers in math and technology, Bartik seized every chance to put her talents to use. During her career, many people overlooked the importance of Bartik's contributions. But as one of the world's first computer programmers, Bartik helped to shape the field for decades to come.

TIMELINE

1924

Betty Jean Jennings is born on December 27 in Gentry County, Missouri.

1941

The United States enters World War II.

1945

Jennings graduates from college. In June Jennings is hired to work on the ENIAC.

1946

Jennings marries Bill Bartik on December 14.

1948

Bartik is hired as a programmer by the Eckert-Mauchly Corporation, where she works on the UNIVAC I and the BINAC.

1967

Bartik receives a master's degree in English from the University of Pennsylvania. Auerbach Publishers hires her to write about computer science.

1997

Bartik is inducted into the Women in Technology International Hall of Fame.

2002

The Jean Jennings Bartik Computing Museum opens.

2008

Bartik receives awards from the Computer History Museum and the Institute of Electrical and Electronics Engineers Computer Society.

2011

Bartik dies on March 23.

SOURCE NOTES

6   Jean Jennings Bartik, *Pioneer Programmer: Jean Jennings Bartik and the Computer That Changed the World* (Kirksville, MO: Truman State University Press, 2013), 39.

12 *Top Secret Rosies: The Female Computers of WWII*, aired 2010 (Arlington, VA: PBS, 2010).

17 Bartik, *Pioneer Programmer: Jean Jennings Bartik and the Computer That Changed the World*, 84.

18 Bartik, *Pioneer Programmer: Jean Jennings Bartik and the Computer That Changed the World*, 22.

28 Janet Abbate, "Oral History: Jean Bartik," *Engineering and Technology History*, August 3, 2001, http://ethw.org/Oral-History:Jean_Bartik.

GLOSSARY

accumulator
a part in a computer where numbers are stored

arsenal
a collection of weapons

ballistics
the science of the motion of a bullet, missile, or bomb

computer
an electronic machine that can store, program, and retrieve data and information

memory
a device in a computer where information is stored

programmer
a person who writes programs, which are sets of instructions for computers to follow

FURTHER INFORMATION

BOOKS

Pelleschi, Andrea. *Mathematician and Computer Scientist Grace Hopper.* Minneapolis: Lerner Publications, 2017. Learn about the life and work of Grace Hopper, another pioneering computer scientist who began her career in the 1940s.

Sande, Warren. *Hello World! Computer Programming for Kids and Other Beginners, Second Edition.* Shelter Island, NY: Manning Publications, 2013. Explore the world of computer programming.

Todd, Kim D. *Jean Jennings Bartik: Computer Pioneer.* Kirksville, MO: Truman State University Press, 2015. Find out more about Jean Bartik's remarkable career.

WEBSITES

Jean Jennings Bartik Computing Museum
http://www.nwmissouri.edu/archives/computing/tour.htm
Explore photo galleries and learn more about Jean Bartik's work as a computer programmer.

Scratch
https://scratch.mit.edu
Learn basic computer programming skills and create your own interactive stories, games, and animations.

Timeline of Computer History
http://www.computerhistory.org/timeline/computers
Learn all about the history of computers.

LERNER

SOURCE™

Expand learning beyond the printed book. Download free, complementary educational resources for this book from our website, www.lerneresource.com.

INDEX

ABOUT THE AUTHOR

Jennifer Reed is an award-winning children's book author. She has published over thirty books for children and loves to write books about interesting people. She has an MFA in writing for children from the Vermont College of Fine Arts.